The Alien Brain Balm

Apply this Balm of symbols freely, or find someone to do it for you …
in whichever order you feel suited.

Poem titles are **BOLD**

Cover image: Brierley-Millman

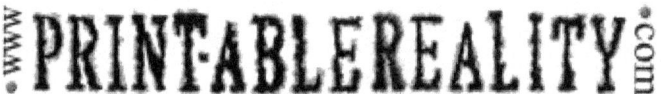

Copyright © 2019   **www.printablereality.com**

ISBN 978-0-473-49765-1

To order copies of this book please email:
gus@printablereality.com

A Way There

Words, those words! Loud - like lyrics that cry to be sung; but he can only read them.

Bell, or ...his silence shaped in to a hunger for noise; soundless and perfect.

Door ... so wanted to be open that he walks around with it; hand in handle.

Secrets ... he could listen to for hours, if only he could stay asleep for that long.

Dreams, those dreams! Matching dreams, mirror dreams, waking-up dreams ...
and waking up-side-down dreams.

And, his hands
without palm lines, like someone's else's reused gloves ... his past ... his destiny ironed away.

Pictures ... of there,
There ... where he wants to be,
like frames for his memory within the image.

Get away if you can, get away
away, away ... far away
get, get, get a way
a way
... get ...
a Way   There.

Another Forever

When we met we met like a kin
When we first-timed we timed for forever

When we sang we sang like love birds
When we danced we danced for surprise

When we trusted we trusted like a naif
When we believed we believed for innocence

When we spun we spun like the earth
When we mooned we mooned for honey

When we touched we touched like parents
When we dreamed we dreamed for angels

When we drove we drove like formula one
When we walked we ran for a marathon

When we played we played like kids
When we slept we slept for babies

When we lived we lived for one another
Suddenly, we die! And yet another

                Forever

passes on.

)auc(K-land   2013

remind me please ...
what is Auckland?
a lot of bush around
and a Krd
...
and maybe a bridge connecting the two ?

A waterfront, corrupted by cranes and containers
lined with bad taste bars, with bad taste music
... and?
and a few other hoods sitting on volcanoes.

An infant child, of a Pacific mother
Europe and Asian fathers ...
growing up a twin of
unwise Oz.

A big comedy, with a lot of smiles
but not enough laughs.
City of sails, that lost the waka.

Eden Park and an A's cup ark,
and Art in the Dark
ages.

A bad carbon copy of a Queen's island into a
Queen street
without a tunnel, or even a concept of being
connected to anything
but a mirror-glass cable, to America.

A kingdom of food courts
with a Warehouse for a castle.

A giant, a hero
who said no! to the nuclear power
and yes, to John Key and Banks !?

A big green and blue sunny postcard
with a lot of white on the flip side
to tell about the rain.

A 100 page map that cannot fit in a book
with all the streets and roads that are,
eventually, no-exit.

A metropolitan-cosmopolitan province
without public transport or public opinion
A menace of a silent gambling tower
and the power of the spoken word.

remind me please ...
what is Auckland?
a lot of bush around
and a Krd
...
and maybe a bridge connecting the two ?

Cartilage

meeting people is like
climbing trees
meeting yourself
is more like planting a forest

trees, trees, trees ...
question mark shaped trees,
growing from
the dots, dots, dots

trees trees trees
in groups of threes:
Mes
myselfes
and Is

trees, trees, trees ... a jungle –
to say:
"I agree, I agree!
only with me"

trees, trees, trees,
woodland of
yous and mes
and the dots ...

there is something burning!
there is something smoking ...
bigger than the trunk of I,
branchy-er than myself,
more rooted than me,
leaf-green, like I am.

it is sweltering ...
Root and Branch
coming out of the pot!
I feel rare, but me? ... me is well done.
I feel raw, but me? ... me is sunny side up.

steaming ignominy!
I cannot see me.
Me cannot see I.
Myself? is not able to spot the difference.
Me known to me, is not nascent
any-more ...
or any-less.

so, I ... and me
plant another tree.

and wait for myself ...

to come,

and climb.

Detritus
(a genetically modified poem in four parts)

I
The Burial of the Following

April might have been the cruelest month
but months are not what they used
to be,
or not to be.
Not months, no memory, not spring
not even
a desire.

Not even.

I asked a little flat rock today:
"What's it like to be dead"?
It laughed at me, flipped in my hand and went
skimming over the water.

I caught a fish a little later
it looked at me with a strange kind of confidence,
while flipping in my hand
as if it was
asking me
the same question.

II
Forgetful snow and other prevailing attitudes

There are things and then there are dynamics of things,
that's what makes them look alive.
Where there are no dynamics
there are statics,
which makes things what they, supposedly, really are.
Alive or dead.

You are following?
... they come into and disappear from your focus.
You think you are following ...
or you are following
your thinking.
Luckily, it never becomes
more complicated

than this!

III
As always, nostalgia forces painful memories to the surface

"Life is short, but the day is too long" – a friend of mine, Eliot - observed once.
Not my days, Eliot! My days are fast, fast like the flicker of a strobe light.
The sun comes like it is catapulted up in the sky, up up up ….
as if darkness was scaring it ... chasing it away from the other side
... reaches the zenith before you even think: morning.
And then falls ponderously on the other side,
snowballing through the evening sky like a comet.
The day dusks down like a giant diving fish,
and crashes ... Sun-sets ... so heavily
that it bends the horizon,
alters the landscape, writes poetry in conflagration ...
the blazing red rock, blind-folding us into the night.

You following?
Following you …

IV
The never seen before, reviewed

Short day! Shortest night. Another flutter
under the shadow of that red rock.
A night called April. In the year of April.
The night you were born.
The night we were all born.
The night life started ...
The night when non-life didn't end.
The night memory began ... The night
nobody remembers anymore
... and that "You",
you who nobody remembers anymore.
The night like any other, you like any other you.
Hypocrite reader, my likeness, my brother!

April, April, April. Says in your birth certificate.
Everything is genetically modified these days,
even months.
Tell her I will bring the horoscope myself
One must be so careful these days.

April, April, April. "That will be carved on to
your little flat tomb-rock".

... whispered the fish as it flew away.

Don't stop at a green light

S.S.S ... Some people stop at a green light
taking the time to remember
cry, inside

inside the intersection
inside of the crossing
inside the inside

T. t . t . t   thoughts ... thoughts …. thoughts
thinking: how long before I can't drive anymore? ...
how long till I even forget my own pin number?

M ... M...M mother ... monochrome ... meditation
scared of people going through the red?
worrying about people who stride in complete darkness?

Plant yourself ... find a place of belonging ...
Put your rubber roots down
Tour parallel universes, naming the stars, create quantum astrology charts

Get from M. m ... m ... to L

L . l . l l ... light ... life ... lost ... lonely ... loony learners

Make pop music out of raindrops, big bangs, and:

Its-green-you-can-cross now-blind-person sounds

Or another significant T

T. t... T - tame unicorns ... love triangles dis-triangulation

Talk while not thinking, and think without talking

And do a lot of that ... tttt

T. (in any case) ...Don't think and drive

Stop! Exercise

Exercise everything, but ignorance

Preach

Preach everything, but ignorance

Calcify

Calcify ignorance

Turn it into a rock or a colour

Like ... Green ..g.g.G ... green ... gate ...ghost

Wait, wait for someone to wipe their windscreen

Look at the rearview mirror, for a long long, long time. Disembodied.

Warmed by the light of the primal eternal elemental ... natural

Take the time to remember:
Remember to be ... B. b. b. b. ... breathe...
I am here and always will be
The space between us
Is permeated with warmth and knowing..
T. t.t.t time...
Well spent, with anticipated tomorrows

E.e. e ... Entangle with me

Some people stop at a green light
Taking the time to remember

Talk talk talk .... be boring
Ask for help .. be annoying
Care care care ... because others DO
Even if you can't feel it sometimes

I know it's like an extreme example of:
"Hey everybody, please don't look over my shoulder while I am doing this,
you can't save me, you can't help me"

... like an extreme case of rebelling against all the expectations,
... control ... authority ... emotional dependency
Yes I know that feeling of guilt
Leading to anxiety .. depression ... suicide
Yes, I know suicide. So what?
I know entropy can't be reversed,
You can't turn smoke and ash back into a tree.
But what when you are ash?
And all you remember is ... smoke.

s.s.s.sss ... S.smoke
Look around, look at others
Use others as mirrors
s.s.s.
S.s.s.s. suffer ... Suffer ... suffer
Nine circles of hell inspection
Emotional weightlifting
Subatomic genealogy exploration
Mapping the way-to-destiny maze park
Take the time to remember

T. T ... I am thinking: "If you are thinking about me as much as I am thinking about you,
you shouldn't be driving""

And you are thinking: what is the sign ... what is the rule ... what is the colour?
and, when there are so many "exceptions to the rule" ... how can any rule be upheld
or even expect any exceptions.

What do you do with your pearls when, it feels, everybody around you just wants to be a pig?
What, when you live in a place, where even pure optimism is not enough?
Land in a world where laughter is THE only currency ... and you can, finally, pay all your bills.

L L L L …. Laughter
Like in that Asimov's "Last Question" -
Put on the mask of non-movement
Blend. Bear it.

Some people stop at a green light
Taking the time to remember

You know that you made it, when your life tells you:
"Sorry for being inconsistent lately".
You can wait now! You can wait...

You can wait ... on yellow, or green or red.

"Hey light, talk to me,

Is yellow a sign that you like me? Is red the sign that you don't? Please wake me up, when you get to green ... Until then you can just talk

T. Talk ..for the sake of it".

Maybe they ran out of fuel. Maybe there is no GTLS signal, hitchhiking their T.t.t ... thoughts ...

The question is: What do you do, when you have nothing to do? Are you safe in your thoughts?

Do your thoughts make people around you

s.s.s safer or suffer? S .. s s?

And some people don't cross

Scared to be crossed

S. Some people stop at a green light

... and nobody even honks

Take the time to remember

Remember harder, remember and keep remembering

How you came to me this morning

And whispered in my ear on an in-breath:

"See you soon".

See you soon

Then ... like in the movie, you see for a moment
That all the lights have gone green
All of them
On all sides of the road
And
That all the green men are lit

Magic spells for the forever generation
... and everybody can go, GO.
YOU can move forward
But they don't
They don't
And you?

       L.   L... L ... L
learn
love
live
last
laugh
let, let!
Let there be light

G.g .g g.
              ... green

find me a word

the bush can't hear the birds
from the noise of thoughts
the deep sea
can't see the fish from the filth
of thoughtlessness

****

find me a word!
find me a word for something
for something that is not connected
and cannot not be not-connected

find me a word for you and me
for you and us
for who you are, and who are we

find me a word for the right path
and the space between markers

find me a word and put it into a bird song
the word, the one word
that stops all the thinking

and then
find me, find me an ear ...
or anything, Anything
that CAN
hear

hear...

you are the labyrinth
and I am a way-finder

I am a leaf
you are the seasons
you are the luck and the shoulder
and I am bird poo flying
you are the spring and the estuary
I am the river
I are a tree
you am the tree-hugger

***

and ... I don't breathe
don't breathe
scared that I will lose your arms around me

you are giving me that
that ... that I didn't ask for, in words

you are giving me, giving me something
that compensates for all gifts not ever received

and I want to give you back more
more, much more then
just myself

****
a hug, a hug making the world
the world, the world I want to live in
***

... today, today the whole world
is a set, for our romance

you knew from the start that this,
this up till now, was not going to work
but it's going to work for what comes next

what comes next?

the fern unfurls ... and I ask you for forgiveness
on behalf of all other lovers

there is nothing so precious as something that has
run its course and knows that - says the falling leaf

the end of living and beginning of love
the end of loving and the beginning of life

forming without the formula
defining without a need for definition

we stick together, we stick we listen we hug
we hug, me and you and she and him and it
all of us ... all
and

the goddess of missed kisses

*excerpts from a stage performance:
"Insomnia in a Daydream"

1.

She lived on a desire island
until the day ...

he swam out of the salty ocean
of all her held-back tears.

He kissed her waterless eyes
her bream-like skin
and let her butterfly out of its frame

She licked him dry
watered his elapsed longings
and pumped blood into his fallow body

I love you, said she.
An island became a mainland
and the mainland became an Eden.

I love you, said he.
As if he remembered her from a previous life
As if he had forgotten Eve's bite.

They wanted it to be slow and fast at the same time.
They wanted to distinguish desires from fears.

So it was;
the sky was a life arch
every walk was a victory march
every road was a high way
they couldn't wait for another day

and days ...
days were dreams
nights everything but sleep
hours were seconds
seconds eternity
... the glory of unity.

She was irresistible. He was resistless.
She grew softer as he grew harder.
She grew in vision as he grew in wisdom.
They found their light-house and they built
the-ir castle.

And then one day she let out her tears
she cried, cried and cried.
Desires grew into fears, fears into desires.

... she cried, cried and cried
just to make it easier for him to swim
... and he didn't kiss her eyes
just swam back to his safe desire-less island.

2.

when I first met you
your eyes, looked like an advertisement
for happiness

when I second met you, I asked: "What is your lucky number" .... "I can make any number happy"

and yes, before I third met you

my numbers came up, number after
number. first time, second time, every time

when I fourth met you
my eyes became video cameras, recording
something to watch while eyes closed

and ... since I fifth met you my eyelashes became
like lips, that just kiss you, kiss, kiss with every blink

before I sixth met you, I rang
your doorbell, and the song of that ring,
still rings, rings ... in my ring

later, at night - when I seventh met you
I opened my eyes and it was dark
you opened your eyes and made a rainbow

when I lost-count-met-you
counting counted for nothing anyway,
my mirror-mirror stopped working

and I can only see myself
... in your eyes

3.

Twilight suburb of a nebula
stars out of constellations
every cloud has a quick-silver lining
night-air is mercury knitted
autumn of the lonely
hermit city in a deep sleep

snoring, roaring
lost in its own mind...

Highway of dreams,
moon pointing the way.

Knocks on my window
moonlight ...
reflection of delight
night-time colour to my day-dreaming.
In the city that is out of its mind, at a time never lost, on track to the well-unknown, to the foretold destination.

At that time,
we're in the same world
The World In Between Dreams.

Sometimes time is the Time
Sometimes time is only a time
At the time when time is everything
we are nothing but timers.
Now, at this time, I sense
we have another, more significant, Now
... to come.

don't be afraid of the past
the past is always beautiful
because it is the past.

4.

This path I travelled today ... from sky to sky
Through the nine circles of heaven

Wandering among your deepest thoughts
... found a shortcut to my dreams

Plunging into your quintessence
I planted my Colours on the hill

Violating the line between tenderness and pain
I crossed the river of my innocence

I will follow
walk down mysterious paths
I inhale your whisper
I walk into my shadow

I hear
Something beautiful
Something so beautiful
Something as yet unwritten -

The Nine Circles of Heaven

If They Ask ...

If they ask me: what is the colour of your eyes?
I'd say: I don't know
must be the colour of the lake,
on top of the hill
... reflecting stones and forest leaves

and, what is that bright, lively beam under your
eyes? the waterfall
a smile grounded in motion
pushing your cheeks up and
whispering,
falling off your
so-kissable lips
winding around your erogenous neck
under the silky-stone-arch of your hair,
over your vertebral column ...

a mounting creek curling down the ridge
... your backbone,
boulder by boulder,
separating and merging
mounds
and the valleys ...
all the way !
to the waves ...
to the oceans

skin captures sun rays ...
sweats

shimmers like a fine-crushed crystal
or is covered by the silvery soft ashes of
your mother

the mountain

if they ask me : what does she look like?
I'd say: I don't know
I only caught a glimpse of her in the eye of an eagle
a flicker image on the wild salmon's skin
a fossil imprint on granite rock
listening in, for her voice - in the wind
of our daughters
singing and playing
.. felt the rhythm and warmth of lava dancing in her
blood,
heart ...
belly
hips
feet ...
clouds and new moon
the hands and wings
springs, roots
moss and needles
twig-light and dusk
falling asleep in the pyjamas of my safe, swinging arms

if they ask :
are we alive?
and, what are we going to make
out of this love?

... are we ever going to be close, be true, to our wild,
naked selves
and unalienable
are we going to be the family
the family we already are
are we ever going to be intimate,
natural
at ease
?

I don't know,
the recording
the history,
can stop
stop and wait
for one day
while I remember you
... from the future

while I try
to save us
from
the future

jet lag

wakes you up at 1.30

to hear the sound of
some other ocean
clearing my ears from in-flight announcements

to stare, to stare at
some other darkness
darkness that is security-scanning my consciousness

.... behind the eyelids
we continue this chess game
and life says: is your move
and I don't
and it ...
It is patient
... genuinely

and I am

and ..... and ... it says: it's your move
(the only time I know I am winning)
and I say: no, I moved, it's your move

what did you move?
I don't remember anymore, but it's your move now

are you sure?

not really

anyway, let's take the board out, to the stage, and continue there
ok, I say - (see, it always finds it ways to make me move)

it's your move, remember, even that there is not many people in the audience, yet

I don't need an audience, you do
you need to move, that's what you need to do
maybe that is just what you need me to do, cos you like playing with me
and the audience
....

there are a lot of people here now ...
do the same rules apply off and on stage?
yes, don't play dumb - play!

after you, sir

you have to move, all your defense lines seem to be open
but ... I am not trying to defend
all your attack lines seem open too
but I am not trying to attack either

do you want to draw then?

no

play ...
come on, you ... just play
you know... I can never win this game

lets go behind the scenes again
continue our piece at the rehearsal room

can you carry the board?
yes, are you bringing all the pieces?
... are you bringing the audience?
bring the patience ... don't move while we are moving

we have everything
play, it whispers
as I fall asleep

... play

John K

there was a boy, a boy from a small island
who lived in a small house with a big screen

a boy who liked fast cars and racing
a boy who never left his island

every morning he would get into his little car
and drive up and down the only road on his island

he knew that road very well, every bump and every curve
he knew that road, so well, as if that's all he knew

when other cars came through the village
he would follow, race, and overtake them - with noise

and stop, and race, and overtake them again
just like big boys, in big cars on a big screen

when the passers-by-car left the village, he would
return to his pole position on either side of the village

celebrating another victory

Living in The(ir) Now

mind your own business
they say, while spying on you

your safety is our first priority
achieved primarily by keeping you in jeopardy

your wellbeing is our first priority too
Ensuring that you are being well uninformed

if you even begin to think that you can grow own food
we will build another shopping mall on your plot of land

if you think you can go off the grid
we will adopt some new by-laws, bills and charges
for your protection

sorry, couldn't finish the roof on the kindergarden
budget run out, had to buy more bombs and grandees

while you thinking of occupying, we will find or invent
another new enemy for you, to keep you occupied

if nature continues to be an impediment to human
consumption increases we will have to further
humanise it

profit-making must perpetuate and sustain
Life? life is optional

all is good !
consumer confidence index
is up 0.02% today

Mandate of Bliss

At sunrise,
I was given one Yes
... and ...
I had no,
no left in me.

One Yes!
And the day is one lifetime of joy.
And the night is one of those things
that
one can not describe by one comparison.

In one word - the wish is granted,
not in form
not in object.
Essence of the vehicle transported us
not where we asked to go,
where we needed to be.

Transmuters,
we overcome speechlessness,
by writing letters to birds and fish.
Florid, luminous, dressed
in the affection garb.

Transmitters,
we invent nothing.
Nothing but a new time,
and a new place.

If the old time had, that one nod,

it would have turned into eternity ...
If the old planet knew what we know
it would have turned into a sun
... a long time ago.

Awaken touch, feel a stroke
of skin, stolen from the morning light,
keeps in the loop ...
touch of dream, spell of love.
Living is the property of the spiral,
the curves have their own prophecy
... turning yes, yes ... turning
following the trace of Mandate of Bliss.

Parting Waves

Perfectly composed nordic stars.
Ocean burning, with white
flames
chasing each other.

A ballad orchestrated by the moon
rumble and thunder
echoes
making crashes rhyme.

Once I held her
in this place
in those arms ...
in palm of my hand:
surfing my life line
breaking the waves
effortlessly,
swiveling ...
carving
infinity signs.

Once... once and future
I thought.
Once ... in this place.
Once no wave,
I thought
can take her.

**

Now I am a just a ripple,
an immaterial quiver

Chasing and waiting
at the same time
a wave between her silent ebbs and tides ...
silent and formless ...

Silence, muteness, quietus ...
demise made to scream only by the starry-eyed
speakers of my feeble memory ...
of my earless heed ...
of my teeth-less hunger ....
of me ...

less and less
of me
hiding from the high seas
eluding the shore.
The life line shorter, straight as an error ...
only my enormous,
Herculian
blind arms clinging more and more on less and less,
hugging the void inside.

I am not there anymore
nor here.
She is not there anymore
not here

she is everywhere.

**

But only
only for a moment
when I am in this place,
I am.

PUSH

there are some beautiful nights
when everything in us sings
pulsates
in an ease of lust
in a harmony of unquestionable, liquid truth
... delight, magic unleashed and proven by a shared experience ...
secrets drowned in a sweat of surprises
our belly buttons tightly buttoned
our skin sensitized and attuned, in a new symphony ...
our whole body laughs ....
pulling this earth
with us
to new universes

I've spent most of my life learning
learning ...
how to unlearn

my intention certainly was - not to make me think, conclude, decide... choose
or make you think
and overthink

My impulsion was,
and is ,
tonight
to give you my time, to hear you, listen in to you,
tune my self-vibration to yours,

play
play the 1000-key-organ that you are

My lips are my hands,
pursuing the limits of senses
... holding on
like a flame to a candle ...
to your body hair
... and goosebumps

as this whole year feels like a conception
like my second birth-year
tonight is my birth-night...
I am slowly,
almost too slowly
coming out
I trespassed all minor roads around ...
and followed the canal to divinity
... the thief that doesn't have to steal anymore
lacking oxygen in this space-suit made of passion

you ...
you are
my chosen mother

the sound of your heart,
the softness of your soul
the smell of your bosom
the taste of your body ...
... those beautiful multi-frequencies of life,
life ...

life given love
love ... let loose
births
new life

seeable is something between visible and invisible
probable is something just short of everything
and nothing is all that is left

Wait !
wait till Mona Lisa blinks
and then
... look at me
with Those eyes
the only gaze I truly recognise ...
tonight, everything is possible
relax ...
relax
take a deep breath

my voice is itchy

nobody loves this world more than me

PUSH !

The Sky Woman, and a Men

Did you hear the story about the Sky Woman ?
She lived in the sky before our time,
and one day she started falling down
don't ask me why.

When I say before our time,
(and this is not meant to rhyme)
this was before there was any land on the planet Earth
just water, an endless masculine ocean,
a perfect mirror of the sky.

So, when birds saw her falling
they called to the fish, and other sea creatures
to somehow make a landing place for her.

And the fish and the sharks. the dolphins and the crabs
dived deep
scooping some mud from the bottom of the ocean
and mounted it on a single little turtle, floating on the surface of the water
for the Sky Woman to land on.

... for my story to begin.

And when the Sky Woman landed
on the piece of mud on the top of the turtle's back
she unleashed her Sky-Woman-ash-coloured hair
and started swinging her hips and shoulders
(now we are talking)
to the songs of the birds

in a creation dance.
As she moved her hips and knees
the mud underneath her feet started spreading
and expanding and expanding
... and that's how all the islands
and, eventually, continents
came to be.

And, that's why we believed for a long time,
that the whole world was carried on the top of a turtle.

Maybe? There is much more to this story ...
But, this is not a story about that Sky Woman.

***

This is a story about the Sky Woman that I met on a
Sky Train going to the airport.

More precisely: a story about other ash-coloured hair
... and a little bit about her eyes
eyes, like endless feminine oceans
... her skin like fathers of the birds
her limbs like dolphins
and the hips that make a mythical-like dance ...
... and stars in my eyes.

This is ... this is a creation story of a different kind!
The story of her hair
the hair, where every fine threadlike strand
is a volume of poetry.

The hair that makes you want to be a brush
or at least a single shampoo bubble, falling down the
drain towards the ocean

the shampoo bubble with a big popping smile.

This is a story about an ash coloured hair,
that looks as if the whole world had to burn down
and return to no-land state,
just to make this hair colour believable ...
beyond any in-flight Sky Magazine
beyond any (re)creation myth.

As if the all the colour of the silver full-moon was
extracted
into quicksilver
and let loose
to fall down on to a turtle she was standing on
onto her head
and create her ash-Sky hair.

Just like that!

... not creating continents
but new moonless skies
and new stars ....

Just like when you look at the full moon
for a long time
and when you close your eyes ...
and the glowing dot mounts itself
into your third eye, into the sky of your lobe.

The colour of the fish skin
seen through the eyes of the shark.
The colour of waiting, exposed to destiny
agony exposed to love
the old landless ocean introduced to the island
the (re)mergence of all the continents to the original

ONE.
Comfortably sitting on the top of the turtle.

The colour of an ageless, shapeless, genderless, beloved,
falling into the arms of an everlasting, universal lovergiving birth to worlds and children, without concept or conception.

The goddess of the gods.

***

She looked at me (of course, I tell this story)
and our eyes invented a new language
the one look that, finally, teaches you that there is no difference between dream and reality
and never was.
The one look that teaches you there is no difference between was and will and never will be.
The look that makes you understand that all the myths and gods and poems and falling(s) in love ARE immortal, true and real.

At one glance, all the countries and continents disappear
and we didn't need passports and departure forms to fill in ... an airport, or a plane ... to fly.

... just a little turtle to land on,
if I ever wanted to.

But that's some
Other Story.

One More Time

as many a time before I looked up
... reached up to the sky,

only to ... to touch the Spring
only to pluck one flower

only this flower
is like a root in the sky,
for the whole blossoming tree

size of the universe

***

stretch your arms, let me feel your clasp
grow your nails I want to wear your scratches
hone your teeth and chew through my fears
reap and bury, my seedless fruit
of glory, guilt and regret

continue climbing, climbing
movement, random and fractal in turn
climb the spring
ascend the sky
rise upon my body tree
plucking up the courage ...
holding on,
loosely,
to my swaying hips

say: you are my ancestor, my cousin, you are my wife
mean it
reach and keep reaching ... and reaching
to something that looks like (and only looks like):
the same flower
the same star, the new something
the new life, made of me
made by you

***

can an elephant, really, climb a tree
has any seed, ever, found its way back to its mother flower
can sounds implode into new meanings
and if they can, who would know what they mean
who would rewrite the script?

I don't know ... and I don't need to know

all I do know is: since my sense of smell slipped over
the curves of this bloom, since my body moulded
around the branches of this bole and
my eyes drowned into yours

the only thing this me exists for is
to see you one more time
just one more time

to see you one more time
just one more time

just one more ...
one more time
more time

Striptease

oneiric ...
invited back
into your memory
like
many times in the past,
unlike
any time before

remembering ...
Involves time-travel,
I take my time and
I put on
my old cloths
so you recognise me

memory ... is taking time
is ... dressing up
and putting on
a make up
on things
that may have happened,
I take mine ... and depart

on my arrival ...
we greet,
beauty and charm
of a memory,
leaves me speechless

more staggering
than any
future
can be

no need for words ...
words ...
words are clothes
worn by our thoughts
so, I strip
leaving my thoughts
naked
letting them go
deep into your
memory

like two flies ...
having sex mid-air
thoughts
are understood,
memory
re-memorised
and yet ...
somehow, it is cold
it's cold, because ..
thoughts are
only
clothes
worn by our feelings.

and feelings?
feelings are

clothes
worn by our instincts

we strip ...

again

and again

this time is different,
seeing you
naked,
totally naked
sends me back
back into
the present

with a memory ..

memory illusive,
like
a smell
of your naked body,
like
a new home
still not built

like an old city,
that forgets its name.

The Lingo

"Yep, just got in. Flight was fine, fine ...
Well, not really, we were bloody delayed in Dubai for over an hour
and they don't even have a separate business class lounge at the terminal there!?
Can you believe it? Yes ....
yes, yes we should defo catch up for a cuppa before conference starts
or, give us a buzz at room 634,
if you wanna have a drink tonight?
Yeah, yep ... yep, catch you soon!"

mmmm
Infusion Hydrantante, pour le visage
Bonnet De Douche
Hillton GEL BAIN
what is this?
DEFENCE HIAR, Dermolenitivo shampoo ultradelicato, senza conservanti, senza glutine
LAIT POUR LE CORPS – finally something in English:
A mega-effective body lotion that instantly soothes and nourishes dehydrated skin, leaving skin feeling soft, smooth and moisturised.

And I, I feel so filthy
someone will have to clean up after me, as
as ...
I was cleaning after people like me-today,
a few years back
when I didn't know
...
the Lingo.

The Look of Love

She was French... or Swiss maybe.
She was a traveler,
a gift from
a friend of a friend.
Brakes on her car didn't work
we almost crashed into somebody
in the liquor-shop car park.
She had a girlfriend
back home, she told me.
She stole a bowl of ketchup
(like, a big bowl) from the restaurant.
The bathroom light
in the hotel didn't work.
We got an upgrade room
and a late check out.

Now ... at midday,
I'm sitting on the sunny balcony
on the top floor
of the highest building in town,
starving.
Bright sunshine bounces of
wrinkled white sheets,
and washes the lines off her face.
She semi-opens her eyes
looks at me.
Her look
looks
as if she loves me
or loves ...
somebody else.
While I was eating last-night's *pommes frites*
colored in red.

The Edge of Your Sword

I fell off the bed
last night ... searching for you

the bed of storm
the bed of wild ocean
the bed of so-called progress
the bed of: you-are-still---you-are- - Just -
-a-millimetre-away.
And the millimetre
the millimetre is filled with a thousand galaxies
with planets, comets and supernovas
overlapping in the continuum of this non-linear time,
non-linear space,
of this non-linear linen

the same linen that Egyptian Pharaohs were wrapped in
to become timeless
the eternity that starts and ends with every fold...
... every sleep-turn.
And it starts again ...
in the next lifetime
every next generation
every preceding so-called civilisation

I started on the left
and you were not there;
so, I moved to the far right ...
Just as any search for justice begins -
naïve, honest, vulnerable, clumsy ...
... search for the collective soul

too far ... so close
and

and the storm stopped
the wild ocean disappeared from underneath my
dream-arch
for one wave
for one lightning
for one fall ….

Oh the gravity! Gravity ...
the reminder of pre-quantum days.
Gravity
hasn't been so painful, since the day of birth

it didn't matter
I was so happy ... so happy
to have found you down on the floor.
Right there ... right and Just
just like everybody's dream
of justice

Right there ...
the pain ...the bliss ... the ache ... the pleasure ...
the sore ... the rapture !!
was like ... ... like I was ripened
ripe by the joy ... of finding you

(or even a thought ... a chance ...a possibility ...
of finding you)

or a thought, just a thought
or a feeling ... a feeling in a dream
in a dream: when blood comes to your eyes ...
in waves,
when the light comes to your eyes ... from the inside ...
and you don't open ... because, you can't ... you can't

open

the dream ... the dream
immortal, perpetual, amaranthine ...
that I could ... I can ... that I will ... that we will ... that WE will
the notion .... unrelieved, incessant, relentless ... of you
coming ... coming ... emerging
with, or without, your unmistakable scales
becoming out of me, made of me
your fairness, my passion
equality, compassion ... even in the dream
is spread ... spread
like an illusionary soft carpet
between me and the concrete floor
between me and a concrete world
...

ohhh
if I were a cactus ... if I were a desert
if I were a turtle ... if I were a dash of wind
if I were the brave one ... if I were the eternal ray of truth
which ... which would I like being the most? Which?

Ohhh ... if I were a slave ... if I were a king
if I were a soldier's wife ... if I were a judge
if I were a whore ... if I were the white house
who? who would I like being the most?
when you arise in me ... Who?
...

space ...
space, I can give

time, I can give
my word, I can give you
love, I can give
freedom, I can give
my world, I can give you
and you don't even need to choose!
Just bring what you have the most.
Kisses made of silence, hugs made of care,
love made of love.
For us to heal ... to hear
to feel the silence ... Just-silence

I hope you feel like India ... before a monsoon
as I feel like a Monsoon ... before the monsoon
before and too soon

I hope you are thirsty ... I hope you are hungry
while I hand-feed wild animals
just to suppress the excitement of meeting you
in your fullness
your blind, measured fierceness

I need a big space between the waves
as I swim towards you
not to catch the breath
but to see
and to catch
the biggest wave
that will splash
that will crash
me
between your tides ...
on to the edge of your sword

my eyes are still closed

not because I am fearful
not because I sleep
or because I reverie.
As you empty my full mind
... and make me mindful.

I am
just ...
just, so I can be blind, virtuous, quiet.
Just, so my minute-of-silence
for intolerance, prejudice, cruelty
can tell
more than many lifetimes of words
... or generations of ideals about you

now that I am Just
a devotee united with his divine, in an act of love.
Just, like you
I want to live, naked and disarmed !
Need no cover, scales or swords

I am barely another carrier
transmitter,
conveyer,
embryo cont-agent.

... she Moon

how are we going to do this?
or ...
how is this going to do us?

Her face reflects the light from the distant stars
shapes our waterscapes and moodscapes
the bright and the fateful, the shapeshifter
the island formed in the estuary of us

how many times do we meet ?
or, do you mean: how many times did we meet?
... how many times will we meet

first time we met
when space and the non-space

last time we met
when separation and unity

first time we met
when dust and stars

last time we met
when water and fire

Don't look for things in obvious places
make it very hard to be found
forget the name that you called me by last
(and my addiction to your skin)
make a new mirror, one that looks completely
different from the one from yesterday
universal intelligence had it all planned

the movement, the stillness, the movement …
the closeness, the distance, the closeness …
the rain … the rain
the orbit and perturbations

Sit there and think how ...
how the lamest things get most of the limelight
where does the bearded guy, that walks up the hill,
come from
when do we meet again?
how does the wind feel, rolling over your face,
playing with your hair
is everything ultimately a chaos or a system,
or a chaotic system,
or systematic chaos
and …
who, who can teach you to play a violin
who?
the violin, the violin

and … we meet again
we meet again,
fated
like the rain and the bow
the Moon and Midheaven
like a girl and the woman and a man and the boy
like tenderness and lust
more, and enough
go and stay

and, all you said was :
"we should not look at a bearded guy, we should look

at the Moon,
the she Moon"

your words ...
sound
that talks directly to chakras
a lotus flower forever open
a poetry
a Goddess,
that needs no prophet or psalms
the Moon
(in his female version)
comes over the Midheaven

The Price of a Gift

around 4am , on my birth-day
a thought wakes me up
a single thought,
thought of you
You, dying in my hands
cell by cell
9 trillion cells of you. Dying
at the rate of one cell per thought...
one kiss per second
one breath per day ...
one gift per life

around 5am, another thought
I clamp all my arms, harder, around you
you ...and your dying cells, all 9 trillion of them,
minus one
and I can smell ... you
... You smell like the future
future. that repeats itself
as we ... sleep-walk and we ... dream-dance,
all around the world
and ... our feet move the earth
to a new sunrise

at 6am
a new thought arrives, together with light
entertains me, fills my lungs
and I hold my breath
and I stop my thought
and I silence my kisses

not to say a word. Not to wake you up

an hour later, you move
your skin feels at home, on mine
... Leaf doesn't find a tree
... Salt doesn't find a teardrop
... Sound doesn't find a violin
They just are ... they just are
they were, are, will be
Living ... and dying. Together

at 8, you open your eyes
the ultimate gamble!
... they remind me of the infinity sign ...
and you close them, quickly
as if you know, that one more cell is gone
as another thought is born
in a blink
that one blink that tells me, in an instant
of all ours previous lives
... next blink
puts me inside a sand clock ...
And turns sand into feathers

time seems to pass?
and I guess, you are awake by now
just morning-dreaming
covered by my no-blink gaze
wrapped in care
Already five cells down
... you look like Monalisa !

... like all my mothers, and all my sisters ...
all my wives, and all my daughters ...
... a stranger, disguised - in a mirror image of myself

your touch travels down my spine ...
like a drop of water on the window glass
like a drop of sperm: in the right tube, at the right
temperature, to the best host, at the perfect time ...
like drops of symbols that write themselves into a poem
like the one word, one that tells many stories
like another dying cell ... yet, another lost thought
like .... another breath, not yet taken
like the first kiss, just to be shared
like ...

the price you pay,
for a gift

The Poetry of Silence and Zeros

To be polite ... to better fit in ... to be worthily
unemployed? Usual answer: in-between jobs.

I am different. What do you do?
I am in-between,
in-between poems.
One that I will never finish and one that I haven't
started... one that nobody will ever read and one that I
failed to memorise ... a long one that never made it
over the page and a short one that got stuck in
graphics ... the rejected one and unsent one ...
the very loud one and many silent ones ... a
confessional one and an obsessional one ... one
amateurish and one professional
... the one that questions the past
and that one that questions the future.

At any unemployment rate, at any point of no interest,
every night and every non pay-day ...
on my screen
there are always two documents open:
the future poem
and a draft budget
for the next poetry project.

Document upon documents
folder upon folders
as large and as empty as my wallet
filled with blank verse and blank excel columns.
The poetry of silence and zeros
in-between

in-between poems.
This one is for you ... (RIP Ian McMillan)

the one who hasn't touched the blue book
but has carved many faces

the one that never made it across to the digital world
the one who didn't search for inspiration or stimulation
from "the cloud", but from the clouds
the one, (no)one couldn't get on the phone
or send him a text

the one who would walk in the rhythm of the waves for months,
in search for an ancient piece of a whale bone
one that would spend months in silence ...
a gentle silent dance with the bone, without power-tools
... one who taught me :how to listen to the silence ...
one who helped me feel and understand,
to the bone ...... and again, spend months walking through the bush and the sand in search of natural fibers, to make a string for a new tiki

one that married the obvious and esoteric
material and spiritual
Maori and Pakeha

one who saw the divine messages in the wood
one who sees the soul ... and the shape of the soul
... one who left a few growth rings on my trunk...
... one who helped me carve around a few life knots...
one who wrote stories and poems with a chisel
one

one with the wood

the one .. and the very last! real bush dweller of
the Auckland city

we all JUST walk by, just walk by, just like a man in
this photo,
by the spirit and the monuments to the spirit, that
(some)one or (no) one can make - like you did

my dearest friend and the Master, there was never
going to be enough time to spend with you ... there is
never going to be the status update big enough to
thank you and love you enough

thanks for the silence, that fills the gap

I hope that my tears help unite you back with the
waves and the clouds

With Out

Her house ... Her living room ...
is non-living.

Tonight, she opens the window.
Chooses The day,
for her Birthday.

What are we made of?
Mind body and nobody.
What can we live without?
Facts built against facts.

All our houses, all our rooms
the Buildings are all ... always,
always "Period Buildings".
The same way we are
just
a sign of what we are going to be
Tomorrow ....
Period.

It's raining again. She pulls the curtain:
"This umbrella is
my house
its grip is my door handle
and I pass
it on to you

to hold."

White and Black

Locked in. White paper, black ink.
I am composing this song.
Black and white piano keys,
to tell me - door to unlock?

... writing this song
one move -
ink spilt,
and those notes remain unwritten,
tear this paper ...
keys locked, sound muted ...
But I must sing!
I must sing!
world to know -
to know what I would not tell.
World to know -
to know what only you know.

... writing?
to tell of something that
can't match up to anything known.
... living?
only like a living place - you are living all over me.
... composing?
blank ink and dark paper, songs hidden in your whisper.
... playing?
my black and white keys of doubt and belief.
... singing?

your whispered orison.

My head slit and my thoughts wrecked ...
now ... can distinguish your glory.
My heart ripped and weakened,
can pump love notes again.

If I was to send you my thoughts,
I would have to send you a mirror.
If I had to send you my songs,
I would have to send you my heart.

I love my solitude, time when I have your company.
You remind me of places out there,
that I haven't been to.
You take me places inside of me,
that I didn't know exist.

In this one citizen state,
on one passenger plane,
on this single man planet,
constantly running away from the moon,
orbiting around You.

Another inner-lock unlocked.
Another knock on Your door.
Another numinous, inexhaustible delight in the religion of love.

Another Day, Another ...

Light - the silence speaking in shadows
... we call it : Morning
when God flicks another token of light
up above the clouds

Another day, we say ...
Another coin

... of light emerges from that dotted darkness
we call : Cosmos

the bottomless pocket of God's small change
... we call: Night
when the moon puts on a mask of the sun,
sometimes half
sometimes just a smile
to entertain us
while God choses a coin
we will call : Tomorrow

Ihumatao

this land   ... is not my land
this land   ... is not your land
this land   ... is not our land
this land   ... is not their land

Ihumatao - the Stonefields, the 800 year old
city of rocks and human steps

the cold nose, sticking out in the harbour
supported by the winds and the stars
and the Mana of those who first landed here

Here! ... at the last stop on the human march, and a
pedal, and a dance   ... from Africa
and The very first footprint on the Land
The Land of the Long White Cloud

this land-scape literally fell down
fell down! hot lava rock by hot rock
from mother earth ... from father sky
just like .... all of us
heartbeat by heartbeat
back to the Mother

and we cannot put anything
anything in between ....
in between:
the Mother and the Father
the Rock and the Rock
the Heart and another Heart
***

we have all come from the ocean
to this land ... To This Land ...

... Hape's waka is still in the harbour!
we came
and confiscated this land

and then ... we came again
to this land...
sail-ships are still in the bay
... and confiscated this land

and we are landing again
again ...
and we want to give it back
give it back!
to us
to ... all of us

this land needs no other:
violation .... colonisation
inconsideration .... annihilation
exploitation .... desperation

this land
this Land has a strong Nation
to protect
To protect it from another confiscation

****

remember, remember
and never forget:
out of this marriage/union
between land and the sky
we were born

not only like brothers and sisters,
but like twins
lookalikes
… like rock to rock
and we just walk the land
until mother takes us back
to make more rocks

this landscape
this landscape has many scars
with many brothers and sisters missing
….
look at the old photograph, compare
look at the mirror
look at your twin
look at yourself
heal the scar
heal the scars on our Maunga

and let mother and father look after us…
mother and father know the best
mother and father know
what's best for their children

***

take off your shoes … take off your shoes!
you are treading on a sacred land

take off your hats
bow to your vows
to protect your path
my path … Our path

… these rocks are our hearts
stacked up
on top of the hearts
 of all
our ancestors

open your eyes … Open your eyes !
look up
listen!
listen to the Rangi
listen to the sunrise and the rain
for the rainbow and thunder
the waves ….
and the waiata of the rocks

better listen
if you don't hear the soft Father's voice,
Mother will speak again

find a rock …. Be the rock!!
one you can take your firm stand on

and know the difference
know the difference between life and …
life and commodity

the difference between value and profit

the difference between convention and heritage

and it doesn't matter the size of the rock
there is no difference between Stonehenge and Stonefields
it's the size of our stand that matters …
the size of your stand
to remind us:
no bulldozers
have tracks designed for those Rocks

no!
no luxury house built
is better than a Home,
home that we already have

pick up a rock
pick up a rock
….
and put it back
where it belongs

Life is ...

Like a walk on the beach
After the storm (or before)

Seeing a piece of seaweed pressed on the sand ...
and thinking : "Christmas tree"
Hearing the birds flying around
Thinking : "I am hungry too"

Seeing an old tree stump
Hard-stamped on to the wet surface, with a
Green leaf attached to it, by the puddle of rainwater...
Thinking: "That is true love"
A bunch of fallen leaves, wet and tired ... spread by
The bush-corner of the beach, in their multicolours
Thinking: "Freedom"

Looking back, and forward, at your own footsteps
(always, the most evocative exercise)
Thinking: "I am so grateful for this life,
For time of solitude and reflection"
A lone little branch
With a single remaining leaf on its top
Like a fallen flag
Thinking: "I am a failure"

Patterns form, as the water crawls towards the surf
Creating a new landscape
Revealing driftwood, rocks and bones
Forming a map

Thinking: "The right path"

A swarm of small fish dominates a newly formed
little harbour, uninterrupted by me jumping over
Thinking: "Evolution"

A lone dog runs towards
It looks joyous, in the moment, in the movement
It will be here in a few seconds ...
Thinking: "Fear"
The owner appears in the distance
Approaches, also running
"Watch out, there is a wasp nest exposed,
Near the estuary entrance"
Thinking: "I wish you were not running
I could do with some company, right now"

Seeing stranded, half dried starfish
Beside the newly formed sand dune
.... Two of them!
Thinking: "This could have been my parents"

Walking far, much further than planned
Looking back to the beach entrance
Thinking: "I should have children...
... and ... did I lock my car?"
Walking even further ... further away
Leaving the grey cloud behind
And forgetting about the car
The parking
The time
Not the children

And all other shoulds

Talking to the ocean ...

How did you survive the storm ?
What would you do differently next time ?
Waves carry the laughter and swell with a fresh giggle
from a mountain creek water
They don't waste time – thinking

The pile of smashed up sea shells are shimmering
Washed with the fresh misty sunshine
... millions of micro, self-reflected greyish rainbows
Printed in the sky, mirroring their shapes and colours
Like wishes
Thinking: "Is Life ... the tide coming in or out?"

Life is
Thinking
Thinking that thinking makes life life
Like a picture frame hanging on the wall

Minus the picture

Stuck in your dream-catcher

Caught like a fly
Can't move ...
Like a wish,
can't make a noise
The feathers around me, make every thought softer
 every feeling more romantic
... Can't even dream

And you
You are fast asleep
Your eyelids doing a long charming blink
Your lashes guardians of dreams

Don't know... if I try to wake you up, and how?
Or just enjoy being idealised for a while

Once you open your eyes
And resume being a responsible socially conditioned
 robotic moving subject
I can continue

Continue
... riding the waves of your boundless imagination
While you grin
Grin and nod
Grin and nod
Grin and nod

Till you fall asleep again ...

Garland from the Plains
(Inspired by "Mountain Wreath" by Vladika Petar Petrovic Njegos)

- I -

My happy days with you,
days on the plains, by the sea.
Dearest ... I am calling you gently ... dearest.
LISTENING IN,
IMAGINING, ANTICIPATING,
DREAMING, WATCHING, FEELING.
I can finish here, enough said.

No! Selfishly I am indulging myself in you,
in every word, every silence,
every morning, every swim and splash,
every breakfast, every walk, smile and dilemma,
every insecurity and determination,
every displeasure, every movement ... every ...
Here, I really should finish.

No, selfishly I am indulging in my happy days.
Before now, I could have dreamed, imagined
and then fantasised, visualised, day-dreamed.
Now I can caress you, tell you stories, please you,
feed you, satisfy you.
I can be with you wherever I want and whenever
I want -consciously, decadently, boundlessly,
extravagantly, multi-meaningly, all day long,
as long as I want ...

From the beginning of time to the end of the world
From the end of the world to the beginning of time.

Me and my happy days, Me and my life-giving love.

I really can finish here,
You understand how happy I am.

Selfishly happy! One happiness, undivided,
happiness from the plains.
With no inbred fears,
no acquired fears.

Those are my happy days with you.
Other days I don't know about,
and I don't want to remember.

- II -

When I lose you for a moment! ...
that lasts for eternity
... I search

I search the distance and I see you:
Your shape, your bearing, your shadow,
your profile. I search the depths and I see
you: Your secrets, your desires, your lusts.
I search the past and I see you:
Your thoughtfulness, your honesty, your warmth.
I search the sky and I see you:
Your beauty, your glow, your charm.
I search the future and I see you:
Your fulfilment, your happiness, your shine.
When I search the emptiness
I see ... That old world,
that world without you.

(and now I really can't stop...)

- III -

Emptiness ...
United emptiness – inside and out,
Emptiness filled with emptiness.

Family lost, Broken parishes, Disunited States,
global Dismaland and the Universe of oxymorons.
Uncurrent currency, utopian justice, implanted
epidemics, distracted distraction, anxiety breath.
Pre-digested truths, spinned realities, soulless music,
fake blues. Love without passion, war without heroism,
slavery to freedom. Empty bed, beat-less heart,
tasteless food... and huge lack of lack of nonsense.

And people ... in a thinking stage with no thoughts.
People ... garish, vast, noisy, cartoon-like,
People with pre-programmed moves.

I get scared, I am hiding, I close my eyes,
I want to escape.
Always the same.
Days are chasing nights,
a race between yesterday, today and tomorrow
all merging together.
And people moving moving moving, without advancing
Different people, without differences.

- IV -

I am rising,
searching for you, calling you.
Dearest ... dearest ... dearest.

I can see you ... you are going to see *Vladika*
yet again, still seeking advice or permission,
confirmation or reassurance.
Like in a dream ... you are in white... in a veil.
You are in white ... *Vladika* is in white,
Yours true white, character white ...
His merely white, like a uniform.

You approach him slowly,
He sits there wisely ... embroidering.
Behind him mountains,
significantly, all-knowingly, bright red;
Behind you the sea or the plains,
innocently, smoothingly, milk-white.
The stone you are standing on is soft,
auspiciously blue.

On your head a veil,
On *Vladika's* head a white hat
Embroidered with a kaleidoscope of letters:

COLOUR-BLIND

Around you both,
people ... garish, vast, noisy, cartoon-like,
People with pre-programmed moves.

I look at them ... I know ...who, when and how
they are going to move, act, react.

You approach humbly,
You speak simply and directly,
You ask your same question reasonably and calmly.

Instead of an answer, as always,
he just hands you his embroidery.

    A white two-headed eagle flies away from his
    shoulder
as if ashamed.

Garish, vast, noisy, cartoon-like people
believe they have just witnessed the ultimate wisdom.

For who knows how many times, you walk away,
lost for words.

- V -

I keep an eye on you from the sky
... to the plains or to the sea?
Go back to white!
Dearest ... dearest ... I am calling you gently.

As if I wanted to wake you up from my dream,
As if ... I knew the answer to your question,
As if ... I can break free from my wings
and my second head.

Swim the plains, run on the sea, touch the sky
And you can give us back our world.

I waited, I am waiting and I will be waiting.
I am here!

On every shore, underneath every stone,
in every forest, behind every cloud.

You know the way … just hurry, hurry.

And don't ever leave me for a second!

Separated –
we exist only as imaginary characters
in an imaginary dream
of an imaginary person.

Wishing Well

The town is
decorated and festive.
You, out late.
I go to sleep
and at once
start dreaming.

In a dream,
I am very tired
and decide to have
a little lie down
... and
in a dream:
I fall asleep
... and
start dreaming.

In the middle of this
beginningless time
I wake up,
next to you.
But not sure if
I woke up from a dream
or from a dream - in a dream?

If only ever, I could be
in two places
at the same time
I would
without doubt
have tried to stay where
I was then.

At that moment,
I see you
by the window,
thinking:
"Who sends people
to people's fantasies?"

Flashing lights light your face
from the outside
... just like
in a dream?

I come closer
and look at the fireworks,
and people
dancing in the streets.

Dream is forever
a piece of fiction,
wandering around
in search of
an awake sleeper
who will make it believable.

"Let's go and join
the celebrations"
you say words,
with my mouth.
"They are opening
a Wishing Well
in town tonight.

Exit Music

...
we took a shortcut across the field,
across and across
afield and afield
not because we are in the hurry
or have to arrive somewhere concrete
(apart from the new beginning)
just because the grass felt so much more
more ....
more inviting, more softer
more nonjudgmental, more allowing
more walkable
than a concrete path
...

www.ingramcontent.com/pod-product-compliance
Lightning Source LLC
Chambersburg PA
CBHW071411290426
44108CB00014B/1784